20FOUR

24/7 I'm learning a life lesson

D'Anthony Jackson

DEDICATION

To my mother. If nobody believed in me, you did! Always. Love you!

CONTENTS

ACKNOWLEDGMENTS

I acknowledge the man above. God I thank you!
Thank you team. If you helped in any way, I consider
you my team and I am thankful.

1
PREFACE

"If one is lucky, a solitary fantasy can totally transform one million realities."

Maya Angelou

It was the summer of 2016 when I decided. I was living in Upper Manhattan in a city called Washington Heights and working in Midtown Manhattan for a very prestigious public relations firm. My commute back and forth to work was about one hour both ways. I definitely had the most interesting times traveling. I was a newcomer to the city and it was my first time calling New York City my home. I had visited the city times before but never for more than a week or so. I prepared myself because I knew the first month would be challenging and trying to say the least. From getting lost, falling asleep on trains, phone dying in the middle of the night, everything was a learning experience. Oh how things have changed!

The train rides were the most interesting because a day never passed by that I didn't encounter a situation that made me think "wow," "aha," or "hmm." From the beat boxers, singers, actors, and all other forms of entertainment to just the regular guy heading to work just like me or the student studying for a test, there was always something that had my attention. Train rides were also my time to meditate, pray silently in my head, and just think. A pair of headphones and some great music on my iPhone was my way of escaping the pandemonium on the trains in the morning and the evenings.

Sometimes I would wear them just so people wouldn't bother me, meaning I would have them in pretending to be listening to music so I could purposely ignore people. I still do this. I remember sitting on the train once and I see these two young ladies get on. They seem to be about 19 or 20 years of age. I'm not sure. You never really can tell peoples age anymore. Honestly, kids look older than me nowadays.

Anyway, I overhear one of the young lady's whisper about me to her friend. They are sitting like two seats away so it wasn't that hard to hear. Of course I had my head phones in but at the time my music wasn't playing so I could hear her. She had no idea. I heard her say, "he's cute. I wonder how old he is?" Her friend responded, "I love the way he dresses too." They then go on this big discussion about the kind of guys they want to date, the way guys dress and all that. It got pretty deep. Now I'm thinking I now know what girls talk about with each other. I was invested in the conversation at this point but not really. They talked about this until the train stops and they get off. I was enjoying the eaves-dropping.

That particular day I wore a mid-blue tailored suit, which kind of explains their thoughts I guess, I'm not sure. However, I don't dress like that everyday so I would hate for them to be disappointed seeing me on days I wasn't coming from work. A small stroke to my ego but what was most interesting about it was the fact that they didn't know I was listening. This made it that much more thought-provoking. The thing about New York is you can see someone one day and never see them again and a year later find out you were neighbors. Funny right? No, its crazy.

I do sometimes wonder what people think of me, how they perceive me, or how they describe me to other people. Don't you? Since I remember, I did. I asked my friend Ryosuke, (Ryo) who was my roommate at the time how he described me to his other friends who hadn't met me? Before he answered, I immediately interrupted him and said, "do you describe me as your black friend?" We are pretty blunt with each other. Ryo is originally from Japan. He laughed and said no but your name kind of makes them question. I pretend to be offended and say "wow, Ryo." Laughing inside. He then go on to say, "no I describe you as a really educated and smart person who knows what he wants out of life." Ryo and I are very similar when it comes to ambition and working towards what we want in life so I appreciated that.

To hear a complete stranger (the girls from the train) discussing me in a positive way in secret (or what they thought was secret) felt like spying but honestly it felt good a little. Although, it was about how I looked versus who I was, it still interested me. I guess my point is, you never know what people are thinking. Its rare that you get to hear someone's real thoughts about you. People have ways of covering their true feelings up. If you ever find someone who tells you the raw truth but they love and respect you, keep them around. That is very rare! Now days, you just have to trust in who you are and know that it's good enough. This simple experience taught me how to be mindful and not to worry much about what people think. It can weigh heavily on you not knowing what a person is thinking but its really not your job.

I learned to take life's lessons to heart early on. I just didn't know how to communicate it then. I remember the details of my life's experiences so vividly and I'll never forget them. That's one of the reasons I decided to document some in this book. I remember all the advice I've been given over the years by my grandparents, my parents, my family, my friends, strangers, and all. I remember how it made me feel and what I learned from not taking heed to a lot of it. They are the reasons I am here today. The lessons I will share here are all moments that have taught, inspired, and enlightened me in some way. I want these lessons that we more than likely share together to inspire you as much as they have me.

It was those crazy train rides and other exciting experiences during that summer in New York that inspired me to write this book. A few months before in February, I started my blog DanthonyJ.com, a lifestyle platform about life, inspiration, style, travel, food, and all the above. It was to simply document my life as I knew it. I'm that friend who takes pictures and videos of everything because I like to have memories and if I don't remember it, I have it documented to remind me. This is the exact reason the book idea came about. My following grew a lot and people were asking me all the time when I was going to start back blogging. I just told them it would be back soon. I shut it down before I made the decision to finish my idea on the book and because I was moving to New York. I wanted to one, save money and two save time. It was hard juggling and I knew I would outwork myself writing the book and running the day-to-day duties for the blog.

Some of the stories I've shared on my blog will be extended upon in this book. I believe I will share things that you've already experienced in life. I also believe I will share things that you have not recognized you have experienced. I like to think I have a way of making people "think". Lets hope this book inspires you in some way. Get ready for a few "aha" moments, a couple of wow moments, and a oh yeah moment here and there!

2

TAKE A LEAP OF FAITH

"If you want to be successful, you have to jump. There's no way around it. When you jump, I can assure that your parachute will not open right away. But if you do not jump, your parachute will never open. If you're safe, you'll never soar."

Steve Harvey

My faith and confidence in myself began when I was a young boy growing up in Goodwater Alabama, a small town that not many people have heard of. I had never heard of it myself until mama got married and we moved there when I was four. Growing up with two parents as pastors of a church and most of my family members being ministers of the gospel and big church goers, faith was something that was branded in me. I read about faith, I learned about faith, my family preached about faith in Jesus. It was apart of my upbringing. And I do believe because of that, I have always believed in God which in turn gave me the confidence and trust to believe in myself.

Sitting on the floor, criss cross applesauce being my 5-year-old self at Goodwater Elementary School, it happened. I remember it. I was in kindergarten and my teacher whose name was Mrs. Johnson at the time was teaching my classmates and I new words. I don't remember the exact word she was teaching us but I knew I could spell it. I thought I was the smartest thing in the classroom. As Mrs. Johnson was talking, of course, I was talking also -- trying to make my friends laugh like always. I remember it so vividly because this time I got caught. I remember her pointing at me and saying "D'Anthony, come here." She then pointed at the board and said to me "teach the class since you have so much to talk about." I grabbed the pointing stick with pride. I completely froze from embarrassment. I was really shame because the entire class was laughing at me and not with me this time.

It was that day I decided. That day I made it my goal to be quite in class, listen, and prove to Mrs. Johnson I was a good student. I learned every word she taught us and I felt as if I could spell them backwards and forwards. The two students who knew the most words and could read the best at the end of the year would graduate valedictorian and salutatorian of the kindergarten class. I thought I knew the most words but God has a really good way of humbling you.

My really good friend at the time Josh knew more words than I did so he was the valedictorian and I was the salutatorian. We both had the opportunity to read to the audience in front of our parents at graduation. That was when believing in myself and speaking things into existence became real for me and it would forever change the course of my life. I didn't know this at the time.

This same faith carried me into very blessed and successful years in my younger life. It was that faith that gave me the confidence to learn how to play piano as a 8th grader with no professional lessons. It gave me the courage to run and become student body president in both high school and college. It was also the reason I applied to graduate school and was accepted and have now graduated. This faith makes me believe I really can do anything. That faith, that belief is what push me every day. I thank God for it every day.

December 16, 2016 I walked across stage to accept my diploma. I remember it like it was yesterday because I still don't believe it happened. The entire ceremony, I was thinking, I can't believe the little black boy from this small town in Alabama with two red lights and a grocery store was about to walk across stage to receive a master's degree at 23. Did it in a year and finished with honors. Nobody else in my high school graduating class had gone back to school for graduate degrees and only a few of us had undergraduate degrees. Applying for graduate school was a leap of faith for me. I didn't think I would be accepted and I sure didn't think I would be able to get it funded but I prayed and I had faith. Not only was I accepted but my degree was paid for in full and I was able to work as a graduate assistant. This itself was a blessing because without that, I wouldn't have been able to afford it without taking out a mass amount of loans.

To receive my degree, I had to do one of two things: a thesis or an internship. I decided I was already doing a lot of research so why not look for internships instead of doing a thesis. I applied for a few local ones but I wanted something bigger. That's when God allowed me to meet one of my mentors, Mr. Bill Imada. Because of Bill I was able to become a cofounder of an organization called the National Millennial Community. With my involvement with this organization, an organization that is changing the way the world sees millennials everyday, I was able to interview Mr. Andy Polansky, the CEO of a prestigious PR firm head quartered in New York City. Through my interview with this individual, I developed a respect for him and the company-- mainly because of there strides toward diversity and inclusion and his personably personality.

My interest for the company grew over time and I eventually applied for an internship - on faith. I've told this story before on Facebook but hear me out. All of the questions came through my head, mainly doubting I would get the opportunity because I was so far away in Mississippi at the time finishing graduate school. That plus an array of other doubts like am I going to be able to compete with other students from top tier universities? Am I the right fit? I really had to get myself together. I reminded myself that life for me so far had been a faith walk and this was only another stepping stone to my purpose. With that inspiration, I applied for a position, sent my resume to Andy, went through the interview process and eventually got the position! I actually got the job!

During this time, I literally fell in love with New York City. I knew I wanted to start my career there but unfortunately I would have to leave and go back to Mississippi after the two-month internship and complete my master's degree. I pondered on whether or not I should go back and finish school or stay and attempt to start working. It was a bit crazy but I really thought hard on it. I prayed for a sign.

One night my friends scheduled a dinner for us all to meet one last time. It was my friends Eljay, Julie, and Veronica. We all were interning at the time. For some reason, there was a big miscommunication about what we were doing exactly so when I get there, they were done eating. Ofcourse, I missed the entire dinner! To this day, they say I was just running late like usual but I don't agree.

My friend Veronica who worked in the same building as me became my coffee buddy at work. Our companies shared the same lobby area. We both interviewed Andy for the National Millennial Community which is how we initially met. The night of the dinner, I think she felt bad for me and offered to hang out with me for a little while. So we walked around the city just chatting. I decide at this point I'm hungry and I see a Shake Shack that so happen to be outside seating only. Ofcourse, my luck it starts to pour down raining. We walk into the McDonalds to get away from the rain. This is when I tell Veronica about what I've been thinking about for a while now. She always has the best advice. She looks at me and she say

"D'Anthony, if you feel like there's something back in Mississippi that you haven't completed, my advice is that you go back and if its meant for you to be back here, it will happen in its time."

This was the sign I prayed for. I needed to hear it come from someone else. She then goes on to tell me about the times she felt that way and what she did. It hit me! She was so right. Every step in my life have been like chapters in a book. When I completed a chapter, I simply said my peace and then moved on in peace. This one was like turmoil because I was moving without completing the chapter. That was one door that God allowed me to walk in and I felt that my work in Hattiesburg Mississippi was unfinished. So I went back and I finished my degree. I graduated in December and then I rested. Yes, I went to sleep, ignored phone calls, and simply rested.

Eventually, I started doing job interviews. Rejection after rejection, an offer here and there, but none were what I was looking for. I wanted to get back to New York but for a while I couldn't find the will power to do it. I made it to the last round of this job I wanted really bad. I beat out all candidates accept one. I knew this was my job. I prayed for it. I clamed it. It was in Atlanta Georgia. The last round was to meet the CEO but I didn't get the offer. I was crushed. For a minute, I asked myself if I was qualified or what the heck was I doing wrong?

I felt like the universe was telling me that's not where I want you to be. I prayed and I talked to God for a few days. I could feel him. I decided the next week I was moving back to New York because I knew that was where I was suppose to be. I get a call from a company I had applied to come in for an interview.

With no job, no money, and lots of faith, I packed my stuff and moved. People ask me all the time, what made you do that? They would tell me that's really courageous of you or you really have a lot of faith. If they didn't say any of that it was because they thought I made a bad decision. Little did they know, I knew it was the right move.

I didn't know what I was doing but I knew what felt right and I did it just like everything else in my life. I've watched God provide for me over and over again and I knew he wasn't going to leave me this time.

I wrote this particular chapter last because I didn't know where I would be at this point in my journey or in my move to New York. I'll tell you. I'm sitting on a train writing this in my notes on my IPhone. I just left from watching a game with a friend at a cool hangout spot. My mind has been racing all day so I wanted to get everything out. This has been a trying month and I don't think I've ever felt more defeated in my life. Every day

I'm praying and asking God was this the right decision. In some way he shows me "YES."

However, since I haven't finalized on a full time position, it's hard to believe. I prayed for a job and I got freelance clients instead. It wasn't exactly what I asked for but it was what I needed and that's how God has showed up for me over my lifetime thus far. As the old saying go "he may not come when you want him but he will be there right on time." He also may not always give you exactly what you ask for but he will give you what you need. I believe that so deeply. So although I want a full time job, God gave me new clients for my own business. I couldn't be more thankful for that.

The day after I landed in the city, I had an interview with a well known public relations agency. I arrived at the office an hour early and I waited patiently for my interviewer to come and get me. She finally walked in. I sit down and I start my interview. I went through about 4 rounds of interviews in less than an hour and a half. It wasn't over yet though.

Two lady's who've both been with this particular company for a few years walks in. They don't say anything about my resume or the work I've done. From the conversation, I gathered that they knew I had the experience so they just wanted to get to know me. One of the interviewers said to me, "why are you applying for this position?" Honestly, I didn't understand what she meant but she seemed very concerned. I go to answer her and come to find out she thought I was over qualified. I just wanted experience and I really admired this company.

She begins talking about another company that I interned at and she said that I know if you made It there, you can make it here. It made me happy to know she seen the work I put in to gain the experience I have but it also made me think. It made me think that I wouldn't get an offer because they thought I was over qualified so like I always do, I begin over-thinking the situation after leaving until I stopped myself. I prayed the next day and I put it in Gods hand. They next day they call me and told me I was perfect for the position and basically verbally offering it to me. I thanked God but I didn't take it. From this, I learned to just do the work and let God handle the rest.

It was because I took the leap of faith and just moved. Trust me! It was faith because I didn't have anything else but my clothes. Because I really believed in myself and in God, I have now scored three clients for my own business, been offered multiple positions, and am waiting to make a decision on others.

My leap of faith isn't your leap of faith and yours isn't mine. I took a leap and moved. Your leap could be to start a dream business or to talk to that friend you fell out with. It's the leap that means the most not what you're leaping at. Is your leap requiring faith? If not, it may not be big enough.

3
TRUST THE PROCESS

"Don't allow your past or present condition to control you. Its just a process that you're going through to get you to your next level."
T.D. Jakes

This is one of my favorite chapters. Of course, I'm a bit bias though. It took me such a long time for this to register within me. As simple as the concept is, it is such a deep one. In all things, there is a process. What do I mean by process? Well, I'll tell you. Process by book is a natural phenomenon marked by gradual changes that lead toward a particular result, the process of growth: a continuing natural or biological activity or function. It also means a series of actions or operations conducting to an end; especially a continuous operation or treatment especially in manufacturing. You could have found this on Google. Let me break it down in my terms.

Take a hot dog for example. It's one of the many foods a lot of people have questioned over the years and it wasn't until I seen the process that it went through to be created with my own eyes that I stop eating them. To be honest, I didn't really like them before seeing this but whatever. They are said to be made with leftover pieces of steak and pork. I don't have a personal quest against hot dogs or anything but even Snoop Dog the rapper mistakenly referred to the so called leftover pieces of meat as sheep wool. Yes, that's how bad it looks!

It is then chopped up to much smaller pieces. Other ingredients are then added to the mix. At this point in the process, it looks like a chocolate milk shake. Yuck! It is then stuffed into tubes and the process goes on and on. What looked like dirty sheep wool at the beginning looked like a yummy hot dog in the end but for that to happen there was a process that even the hot dog had to go through.

In life I refer to a process as the time of preparation to get something from one place to another or change something. It is a time of learning, a time of transitioning, a time of actions, and so much more. It is the time when you are changing and sometimes you don't notice it as a process until after you've come out of it. I feel like I always knew this but I didn't always have the language to communicate it.

We sometimes ask the universe for things that we are not prepared to handle whether that be physically, mentally, financially, or all the above. I really believe when we proposition the universe or pray to God for something, we have to be prepared to go through what we need to go through to get what we asked. For instance when I asked God for wisdom, instead of wisdom he put me in situations to be wise in. From the situation or the process, I learned wisdom which is a lot harder but worth it. I even thought I wanted more faith. I mean really who in there right minds do some of the things I've done without faith? Seriously, I even ask myself. I was then put into multiple situations where I had to rely deeply and depend on nothing but faith, like my transition to a new city. Its tough but I understand that I am in the process to something that I asked for a long time ago. With that clarity, I can be content and go through my process.

You see? It's a small piece of how this universe works. This is not to make you think twice about what you pray about or ask the universe for but it's to make you ask yourself, do you want to go through the process to get what you are asking for? Its almost a give and take situation. What are you willing to give to receive?

When I say all things I mean just that. If you don't endure a process directly, you will endure it indirectly. I believe this. I always knew in life we go through things and because of that we learn so much from it. However, my belief is that when you ask of something from the universe or from God, you also ask to endure something to get it. I don't believe anything is free. You just pay for it different ways.

My friend and roommate Eljay said to me one day that he felt like there was something more that he should be doing on this earth which sparked a conversation about "the process".

He knows I'm writing this book so I told him my perspective on "the process," since at the time I was writing this chapter. I explained how sometimes the things we go through correlates with that feeling. That feeling that there's more for us to do here than what were already doing. My understanding of this concept is what makes me so content with my life right now. I explain to him that I have grown to be content in the process even though it can be so uncomfortable. I don't think I would be so comfortable struggling with things if I didn't understand this.

A good friend of mine and fraternity brother, Dondraius who right now is a law student in Texas, said something so key for me. I quote him because when he said it, it registered with why I do a lot of what I do. He said in a Facebook status one afternoon that,

"I am motivated to place my family in a different socioeconomic status, whether that's by example or actual financial contribution."

I was never able to put into words what I wanted to do ultimately but when I read this, it clicked. I believe, because of this I have to do a few unconventional things to get to where I am trying to get to -- like moving to New York with no job or write a book with hopes to inspire just one person instead of selling it to a thousand.

I really begin to understand the meaning of "the process" and how it correlates with your supreme destiny in life through one of my pastors, Lucinda White, who is a stellar story teller and dynamic international minister. I've heard her minister all of my life and as many times as I've heard her tell her story about her woods experience, I get something new from it. Her woods experience was a process for her and it was where she said God sent her to prepare her for her destiny. Every sermon and service I would hear this story and each time, I would take a different nugget home with me. She said something that really stuck with me for a while. She said,

"The process can sometimes be a killing field."

Nothing in the world could make me understand what she meant by this. I meditated on it for a while and I realized she meant the process is just a time of preparation. Sometimes God takes you through a process to prepare you. During this time, you have to kill some things or get rid of some things that are hindering you from getting you to your next level in life or career. For me, it has been pride. I still struggle with it and it is one of those things that I am fighting in my process. Ask yourself, what am I fighting in the process?

4
PREPERATION

"If people knew how hard I had to work to gain my mastery, it wouldn't seem wonderful at all."

Michelangelo

I think the quote above is a testament to how we all feel sometimes. People around you see the blessings and wonder how you're so blessed but they don't wait to hear how you made it over. A good friend and fraternity brother of mine Jaylen Hackett said to me one day

"just because I don't broadcast all my wins and losses don't mean I don't lose."

I looked at him and thought , that's it! Yes, that's it! People think that because you don't talk about every time you lose, you don't lose.

They only see your blessed moments. I claimed that as a "tweeting moment". I tweeted it immediately and tagged him in it. We were sitting in Starbucks catching up at the time. That's also the thing with social media. It has created this false reality that everyone's lives are perfect. Yes, in some way we are all blessed. We are simply blessed to be here but what's most important is to show people that life hasn't always been this way. I struggle. I lose and because of that I can win. That's why I write this book to show people life can be an abundant of blessings but sometimes you have to endure some things on this earth that's not so instagramable or tweetable. You just have to go through the process, learn everything you can from it, and tell your story to the next person.

I remind people that behind every glory, there is always a story. You just have to take the time to listen to them. Every person has a story of how they made it where they are now. Even peaches and cream went through a process to be prepared to taste oh so good. Sometimes a story of multiple failures before one success, sometimes sickness, and even worse, death. Its during those dark days that we have to learn to prepare. I thought hard on writing this chapter because I didn't know if I had much to say. I then thought how could I forget, at this very moment, I'm going through one of those times in my life that patience is a virtue.

It's the interview process with companies trying to finalize on the perfect job. Over the past few months, I've had probably 50 plus interviews. Some I purposely took for practice, others I really wanted to work for the company, and others I just wanted to see if I was qualified and liked enough to get an offer. After multiple offers, multiple rejections, and all that I begin to prepare for my future. The whole time, I was asking God to give me a job but instead he was giving me time to prepare. Not only prepare for what I am asking for right now but prepare for my future. I had to learn to look at the bigger picture.

That's exactly what I did. I begin to get myself together inwardly and somehow, my name begin to float around the city. I begin to get calls and emails about doing public relations and digital work for small businesses and companies. I didn't know how to take this because this wasn't what I remember praying for. I then remembered that I prayed for my own business a while back and I didn't say when. I got my first New York City client who I simply describe as amazing. She is known as one of the best career counselors in the city. She has since become like a mentor to me.

A friend of hers who is the CEO of a Market research company also needed help with some of the same things and a number of other projects. Her company became my second client. I am blessed to be working with such an amazing group of people. This was all a sign and it was all happening really fast. God was looking out for me in a way that I couldn't recognize until I really thought about it. He was allowing me to do the work I was passionate about on my own time and still leaving me room to prepare for other things. Preparation is important. There's only a few things in this world you can do well without preparation.

I had to take a step back because I felt like everything was happening so fast. My second client told me about another colleague and friend who was looking for someone to do the same thing. This person ran a business focused on spreading positivity in the world. Her story was beautiful. She made stickers and she ran a number of successful social media accounts. She needed help growing the business and organizing it a bit. All this was happening in less than two weeks. I asked myself before I spoke with this potential client, do I accept a third client or do I wait to see if I'm going to accept a full-time position. It was a big decision because I thought with my client list growing so fast, I don't want to accept a job and not be able to fulfill all the obligations I've promised. I then started pondering on should I end my job search now or should I take one of the offers I've received and work my business part-time.

At this point, I've interviewed with top tier news outlets, top-tier PR firms, and a number of New York based marketing firms. I've received verbal offers, offers on paper, I've even been offered the job on the spot. None were what I really wanted. I thought I wanted them because I needed a job. God was still saying be patient and prepare. I didn't know what he was saying prepare for but now I know.

It couldn't have come at a perfect time. I was

sitting on my friends couch working on some things for one of my clients and I just paused. I said to myself "I am doing too much, just relax and take in this moment." I needed that. I simply looked out the window and said "Thank You." Not long after that my phone vibrates and it was an email from the HR recruiter at the job I had been interviewing for, prayed for, and wanted really bad. She was emailing to set up a call. I immediately thought I was getting that "we thought you were great but decided to move on with someone else" call. I was preparing for it. Not this time. Nope! I finally got the job offer I'd been praying for!

With so much going on, I begin to get a little distracted but I was reminded that remaining focused was the key to my success.

5
REMAIN FOCUSED

"The key to your success is to remain focused."

Paul Beard

When I moved to Hattiesburg Mississippi for graduate school at The University of Southern Mississippi (USM) in August of 2016, one of my first goals was to find a church to attend. Knowing how many church's exist, I knew this was going to be a challenge. While I was at The University of West Alabama (UWA), It was easy for me to drive home to church because we were so close. It was about a 35 to 40 minute drive so I went to church often.

Honestly, I grew up going to church three days a week and sometimes four for years it was all I knew. In the south, I feel like there's a church on every corner. Literally, the street I lived on had two churches across the street from each other and they looked just alike. That's another talk for another day though. I just wanted a place to go to on Sunday's or throughout the week that would be fulfilling. Church service to me was like refilling for gas for the week and I needed that booster, especially in graduate school.

My pastors from home, Pastor Richard and Lucinda White who also happen to be my uncle and aunt told me about this church called Dominion and Power. They always look out for me. I had heard the pastor there minister before so I was really excited about going to visit. I remember seeing the church Facebook page post about a service one night. I decided I was going to attend. I write about my schedule for that day for class, meetings, and appointments because I wanted to make sure I was on time. It worked out perfect. I got dressed for my last meeting which was late and I wore what I had on to the service.

I get there right on time, sneak in, and purposely found a seat in the back so I could sneak back out without being noticed. Sometimes I just didn't want to be noticed. The pastors there are friends with my pastors so they knew I would be attending one day but they didn't know when. The word for the night was about favor. I felt like everything he was saying was to me and I couldn't control my emotions. It was really good and I knew God was speaking to me through him. When the service was getting near the end, I grabbed my bible and keys and was prepared to sneak out. It was so funny because I kept eyeing the lady at the door. I bet she was wondering why. That's when it happened. The pastor, Apostle Paul Beard points at me and asks me to come to him. I point at myself as if he could have been talking about the wall behind me. I really didn't want to go up.

I walk up and he begin to prophesy and pray over me. He begin to say a lot of things that were like triggers to me. He told me how successful I would become, my dream of building someone a new home will become a reality, and lots of other things that only I had talked to God about. I knew it was God speaking through him because no one knew this stuff but me and God. I only prayed about these things. I was in awe and I could feel Gods presence so deeply. Out of all the things he said to me, one thing stuck with me the most. It was so simple. Really slow he said,

"The Key to your success is to remain focused."

This was so key because at the time I was allowing a situation to distract me from my ultimate goal at the time. When he said it, I blacked out for a few minutes because it sounded like it was coming straight from the mouth of God. If I had the ability to imagine what that sounded like. It was more of a feeling.

I already knew this and I had heard this a million times but when he said it, it clicked. To this day I don't know why exactly. I know that I am a focused person and because of that I have so many distractions that come my way to try and make me lose focus.

Remaining focus has been one of the key traits I credit to my success thus far. Distractions come in so many forms: family, friends, hobbies, addictions, relationships, colleagues, and the list go on. It depends on what you're vulnerable to or what takes priority in your life because of vulnerability. It's anything that in some way takes your mind and spirit off of your ultimate goal(s). The key is to learn what things you're easily distracted by. This way you know what you are battling against. It took a while to learn this but because of it, I am on a much better life journey.

6
GRATITUDE

"The presence of problems should not rob
you of the feeling of gratitude"
T.D. Jakes

When I was getting ready to start writing this
chapter, I had just heard about my friend who
had been admitted into DUKE University
hospital. I dedicate this chapter to her, Libby
Hankins, a person who really embodied what
real gratitude meant. I mean it with my whole
heart when I say she taught me so much. I
remember when we first met. We were both
freshman at The University of West Alabama
(UWA), a college in this small town called
Livingston. She was from Gordo and I was
from Linden – both really rural Alabama
towns, so it was nothing new for either of us.
One day, on my way to band prep for a
football game - this small, blonde, happy girl

walks onto the elevator where I am. It was just her and I. She looks at me with these big eyes and smile. That's all she did! I could feel the positive energy from her. She had a cheerleader uniform on and a white bow on the top of her head. We introduced ourselves to each other and went by our way.

A few days later, I get an assignment from the editor of MUSE, the university newspaper. I had just began as a contributor, writing stories and taking photos. My assignment for the next issue was to find an athlete and write a story about them. Unfortunately, I didn't know many athletes or many people at the time since I was only a freshman. However, I remembered meeting this girl on the elevator. My only problem was that I wasn't sure if my editor considered cheerleading a sport. This was always a debate since I became friends with a number of the cheerleaders over the years. Come to find out, she did! I just wanted to find the first person I could so I could get the story completed and turned in on time. At the time, I didn't care who it was because I just wanted to publish a good story. So happen, I had just met Libby so it worked out perfect. It was destiny.

I didn't know when I would see her again and I didn't want to knock on her door so I just hoped I would run into her again soon since we both lived in the same dormitory (Stickney Hall). One day, heading to my car, her and a few of her teammates were walking out of the dorm. I ran over to her and told her I wanted to do a story on her for the school newspaper. She was more excited than me!

I let her know it would take a few hours since I needed to sit down, interview her, and take a few pictures around campus. She didn't care, she was super excited and so was I. It was my first real story to be published and I had just started working for the paper so I wanted it to be good. We sit down and and start the interview. I remember it so well. We were in Stickney Hall Lobby at the time. She told me how much fun she had cheering, her time in Gordo, what she would have done if she didn't attend UWA, and so many other great things.

She then tell me something that I would have never even possibly guessed. She tell me she had been diagnosed with Cystic Fibrosis (CF) since she was two years old. Honestly, I had no idea what it was. I just assumed it wasn't good. She explained to me what it was and how she dealt with it everyday. It's a progressive, genetic disease that causes persistent lung infections and limits the ability to breathe over time. In people with CF, a defective gene causes a thick, buildup of mucus in the lungs, pancreas and other organs. In the lungs, the mucus clogs the airways and traps bacteria leading to infections, extensive lung damage and eventually, respiratory failure. She was like an expert on it. I mean she had lived with it then for more than twenty years. I immediately fell in love with her zest for life. She was thankful for every breath and now I know why.

When she told me, I almost told her she was kidding because she never mentioned it. She didn't really tell people. Plus, she was so happy and seem so healthy. She was all of that and she was so thankful for life. She showed it through her smile and the way she made people feel about themselves. I was so invested in knowing more at this point. What I thought was just going to be story about a freshman athlete turned into an amazing inspiration to my life and thousands of other people. I wanted to know more, even after our interview. I wanted to know what made her so happy? Why she pushed so hard to be successful? How many people did she know with this illness? I had so many questions, even though I had already asked her so many.

These were all questions that I would eventually get to ask after becoming friends with her not long after. From multiple hospital visits, a number of surgeries and procedures, taking medication everyday for her whole life, how could a person be so happy, thankful, and have such gratitude? I really wanted to know. She credited her support system and the love of God for her ambition and drive to remain so happy and thankful even with such a chronic disease. I remember her saying a few times before that

"I have CF, CF don't have me."

And for this I never complained again. It was two weeks after my transition to New York when I found out Libby was back in the hospital and was not doing well. I immediately go into prayer like I always do. I send her a text every time she had a hospital visit to let her know I was praying and thinking about her. I may not get a text back immediately but I knew when she was feeling well, I would get a text back so this time I sent her a text that said the same thing with a photo we took together at homecoming. She was the outgoing homecoming queen and I was SGA President at our university. My phone buzzed a few hours later and my heart just gets really happy. I thought it was her but it was her wonderful mom Susan letting me know that Libby loved me and to continue praying for a miracle. A miracle was all I knew because I knew she was going to fight this and we were going to see each other soon. A little over a week later, Libby makes her transition into heaven. It would be selfish of me to ask God why he took such a jewel so soon but heaven was so fit for a person like her. She was the epitome of gratitude. I never met a person who appreciated life so much and I am so happy to dedicate this chapter to her.

I see gratitude as a payment. It pays more than money can. A simple thanks can make a persons day. A smile to show that you are happy to see a person is another form of gratitude. It exuberates from within. Gratitude and other things like worry and excuses cannot dwell together. You must choose. For this, I choose to be grateful.

Because of this lesson of gratitude, complaining has become one of my all time pet peeves because it is a drawn out way of making an excuse. It never solves a problem, it just forces you to dwell on it and it commands negative attention and energy. When I find myself desiring to complain, I think about how many other people are going through something worse than what I'm dealing with and yes there are thousands of people who are battling something worse than you. Look for ways to show gratitude when you want to complain. It will be hard but in the end it will be worth it. Ask Libby!

7
PATIENCE IS THE KEY

"A man who is the master of patience is master of everything else"
George Savile

I remember it like it was yesterday. Everyday after school, my older brother Derius and I would finish our homework, clean up, then set out to feed the animals before it was too late to shoot basketball. That was our daily routine. I'm not even sure if he remembers this. We had pigs, chickens, roosters, our dogs, the neighbors dogs, stray cats, and eight feet way from our home was a huge cow pastor with every color cow you can think of and one gigantic bull. We pretty much lived on a farm, we just didn't have a red barn. People still don't believe me when I say this. This time in my life taught me the importance of patience and it has carried me until now.

Each animal had its way of teaching me a lesson about patience. Every day after school when we would go down into the woods to feed the animals, I would hope the chickens would have laid eggs. No one knew it but I really looked forward to it. It intrigued me for some reason. I would think, how does this round, hard object come out of this little soft animal. Remember I was a kid then. Weeks would go by and we wouldn't see but a egg or two then we would go out and almost every chicken had laid an egg. It was never on a regulated time that they would lay them so you would really have to be patient with them. Especially me because I was always expecting it.

◆

The one thing I hated about having farm animals was having to deal with how disgusting pigs/hogs were. They were stinky and they lived in mud. We would clean their pins out and ten minutes later they would have created another mud puddle and messed it back up. Its so hard to deal with something or someone that you're not fond of. This was my relationship with pigs. I literally had to deal with them because it was my chore every day to make sure they were fed. They taught me how to show love to those things I didn't really like. I now appreciate them. I actually wouldn't mind having a few of my own one day. If only my younger self could hear me now.

The animals that I absolutely loved was our dogs. We had a girl name Crystal who was a full blooded pit bull. She was as smart and athletic as could be. I remember walking outside every morning to walk to the bus and she would be jumping into the air about three to four feet off the ground because she was so excited to see us. She was family. As much as my parents hated it at the time, we loved it when Crystal got pregnant by a stray because we knew that meant that there were going to be a lot of little puppies to play with every day after school. We waited and we waited. Every day and every week we would be waiting to see when she would birth them. I felt like we waited for so freaking long. Eventually she had eight beautiful puppies that we loved until we had to give them all away to family and friends. In this situation, being patient was worth it but that's not always the case.

My step father at the time was a carpenter and he always took us with him on the weekends and during our summer breaks to help him with his projects. That could be building a house, a garage, or replacing windows and doors. These projects lasted for weeks and sometimes months. We would wake up in the morning, go to work, and work until really late at night. This would go on for a while. I didn't realize how much I was learning from these projects until later in life. I just wanted to see the finish product. I didn't care about making sure it was right. I didn't care about putting in insolation so the house wouldn't be cold in the winter. I wanted to stand in front of the house and say wow we did that! I didn't realize it would take so long. This taught me the most patience. It taught me that it takes time for something to become so beautiful and to be so complete.

After taking a leap of faith, going through the process, remaining focused, and being thankful, you've done your job. Now its time to let God do his. Its your time to sit back and be patient. Like the old saying go,

"He may not come when you want him but he'll be there right on time."

My friend Jasmine whose now in California says this a lot. I know this to be true. The universe have a way of allowing things to happen to you right in the perfect timing. I've wanted to give up on my dreams before. I've said it out loud "I give up." It was in that thought and that split second when my prayers would begin to manifest. It could be a bit scary because it makes you wonder, why a person have to get to that point in there life to see a turning point.

Patience teaches you many things. It teaches you the importance of having to wait for something that you desire really bad. It teaches you humility because you realize you're not always in control because if you was, you would make it happen immediately. It teaches you love and so many other things. Patience is the key that unlocks everything else. You've done everything else, now you just have to wait and send out positive energy.

8

THE POWER OF ENERGY

"For in Him we live and move and have our being."

Acts 17:28

This is the scripture Oprah said she would repeat over and over to herself when all the commotion was surrounding her new network OWN, the Oprah Winfrey Network. She said everywhere she turned there was another negative headline about what was happening with the network and what she should or could have done differently. She then said something really key. She said,

"If you allow the external forces of everybody's else's energy to enter into your own consciousness, it could really bring you down."

This was like revelation to me. I remember thinking back to when I was younger again.

Back then, if someone said something negative about me, I'd pretended it didn't bother me, then I would say something worse about them, ignore them for a long time, and then go by my way while that thing ate me up inside. I carried that energy in and around me because I allowed it. On the phone one night, talking about energy, a good friend and fraternity brother of mine, Dexter Thornton said to me that

"negative energy is like sinking sand."

I responded with WOW not just because of the quote but because at the time I was finishing this chapter. He had no idea. Think about that. Just say you've spent your entire day being positive, loving and appreciating life. One thing happens and in a split second your energy level goes down and you become sad or down. This is why the power of energy is so important and the great thing about it is that you have complete control over it.

I begin to learn this early on in life and how vital it was to forgive people. No matter how bad they hurt you, forgive them. Holding the grudge or that hate is like a dark rainy cloud over your head while they bathe in the sun. I tell people when it comes to forgiveness, you have to be a bit selfish. Forgiveness is not for the other person, its for you. Now, while I don't notify a person letting them know I forgave them don't mean that's the route you should take. I release them so I can release myself. As soon as I do that, I watch how the energies around me begin to line up. It goes back to the process. This doesn't happen overnight but it takes a first step.

From a young age, I could feel this thing in me. This thing like a presence or a voice telling me there's more, even when I felt like I had accomplished or reached my ultimate level of happiness in life. I could feel it, I could hear it, but I couldn't see it. Even today, I feel it pulling me saying there's more for you than you know. You just have to keep reaching. There's just one thing I had to concur. Fear. Fear which brings doubt were the things I struggled with like us all. To be frank, the doubt wasn't my doubt, it was the doubt of other people. There energy had a way of effecting my life. I gave them that control.

The way I've learned the world operates is by waves. Waves could be thoughts, sound, prayer, meditation, emotion, etc. All of these have one thing in common -- energy! Whatever you put into the world is what you get out of it-- even if it's years down the road or the next few minutes. I've always knew this, I just didn't know how to communicate it.

Every morning, I wake up and I say a prayer to let God know how thankful I am for allowing me to see another day. I am not worthy. I then sit in silence and think on where I am in my life. Sometimes I lose track of time doing it. When I don't find this alone time to meditate, pray, and just nourish my relationship with God, I feel lost. It all falls back to energy. Aligning my thoughts with what I want and what I am meditating and praying about I believe sends out a positive signal into the universe. When all of this is in alignment, I can feel it, I can see it. I feel so powerful. With that being said, I am far from perfect but I am grateful that I am allowed to experience how good God really is. It's a time of gratitude and thoughtfulness.

When I was a small boy, my grandmother Peggy every Wednesday would get all the kids in the church and teach us a new bible chapter. I learned from Genesis to Corinthians and I don't remember learning anything else. Everything else I learned on my own. There was this one scripture that stuck with me. It said,

"meditate on him day and night."

She passed around the time my younger brother Elisha was born and the scripture still sits with me. Now, when I meditate, I think about her. I can still feel her energy around me. Her death was the first hurt that I ever felt in that way so I am often pondering on that day. It's the same with my grandfather and grandmother William and Daisy Jackson. I feel their energy around me in trying times. I remember Dr. Maya Angelou talking about how she take her ancestors into meeting and things with her. I caught on to that concept fast. I now walk with my hands down as if I'm holding two other hands within mine and I imagine every step of the way my grandparents ancestors, deceased friends are all with me because I cant do it alone. I placed this chapter last because I have so much more I want to say about the power of energy. My hope is that this makes you want to read the next book. It will cover more topics on its importance.

Let your energy walk before you. It will speak when you can't speak. It will do what you can't do. It will if you won't. It can if you can't.

D'Anthony

———

Made in the USA
Columbia, SC
12 May 2017